How to Get EXPLODING REFERRALS Through Networking

Copyright and Disclaimers

How to Get Exploding Referrals

Copyright © 2018 Port Bell, Inc.

Thank you for buying an authorized edition of this book. All rights reserved. No part of this publication may be reproduced, stored in a retrieval system, distributed or transmitted in any form or by any means, including photocopying, recording, or other electronic or mechanical methods, without the prior written permission of the publisher, except in the case of brief quotations embodied in critical reviews and certain other noncommercial uses permitted by copyright law. This document uses trademarked names of other companies. Use of these names complies with trademark laws. All product and company names are trademarks™ or registered® trademarks of their respective holders. Use of them does not imply any affiliation with or endorsement by them.

For permission requests, write to the publisher, addressed "Attention: Permissions Coordinator," at the address below.

Port Bell, Inc.
2602 S 38th St #361
Tacoma WA 98409
www.portbell.com

First edition: August 2018

How to Get EXPLODING REFERRALS Through Networking

www.explodingreferrals.com

by Dr. Ty Belknap

Table of Contents

Introduction 4

101 - New to Networking 8
    What is a referral? 10
    Two Kinds of Referrals 11
    Three Types of Networking Groups 13
    Getting Referrals 16
    Presentations 18
    Elevator Speeches 21
    Summary 23

Beginning Networking for Introverts 25

202 - Advanced Networking 28
    Giving Referrals 29
    Asking For Referrals 31
    Who do you know? 33

Super-Secret Squirrel 42

The #1 Way to Get Exploding Referrals 46

Conclusion 48

Introduction

I was coaching a client who had decided to join some referral networking groups in order to get the word out about her business. She attended every meeting for six months, but she had not gotten a single referral; she was starting to get frustrated with the process.

We determined that she was having some trouble figuring out how to get her referral needs across and I understand her frustration; I've been there myself. I've been an entrepreneur and business owner for over 20 years and in that time I've joined networking groups, chambers of commerce, social groups, masterminds, etc. But, like the person I coached, I sometimes had a difficult time getting referrals.

I'm now a success coach with Port Bell Business Coaching. I am a Doctor of Strategic Leadership with a concentration in Coaching and I'm a certified coach through the International Coach Federation. I don't tell you this to impress you. Even with my degrees and certifications showing I was a professional, I still sometimes had trouble getting referrals.

Then I realized that I could use the specialized coaching techniques that I've been taught to get more referrals and better-qualified referrals, so I developed a system.

I'm sure you've developed systems yourself before. Maybe it was a system on better designing your kitchen for meal prep, a new way to market your product, or just rescheduling your time. Those are all systems. And it's common knowledge that it can take some time to master a new system.

A new system could even be like a new golf swing or tennis swing; sometimes you even get a little bit worse before you get better.

But not so with this system.

Every person I've taught this system to has immediately gotten better results; sometimes two or even five times as many results in referrals as before.

A network marketing friend went to three different referral groups each week (12 meetings a month), and averaged five referrals a month.

I taught this system to him and he started getting up to ten referrals a week immediately after he implemented it. And he was closing twice the referrals from before since they were better-qualified referrals.

I originally set Exploding Referrals up as a webinar. And, since you purchased this book, you will have access to a recording of the original webinar. But this book contains a lot more than the webinar, so be sure to read it.

This book will show you how to get exploding results through network marketing groups and it will be faster and easier than you've ever done it before. And the best thing: It's easy; it's not rocket science, it's not brain surgery and trust me, you do not have to get a doctorate to be able to use this system.

I'll show you how to get 3 to 5 referrals with every 1 to 1 you do. You can implement the system in your 8 to 10-minute speeches, and best of all you can even use this system in your 30-second elevator speeches.

And don't worry; I'll explain these terms as well just in case you are new to referral networking.

101 - New to Networking

So Welcome to Exploding Referrals! If you were looking for the pessimist support group, I'm afraid it's been canceled; nobody thought it would work.

Oh and surprise, surprise: The underwater basket weaving class has been moved to the pool.

This is exploding referrals. You are in the right place whether you are new to networking groups or if you have been around for years. The only requirement: You want more qualified referrals from your networking groups.

This is not about network marketing. This is about getting referrals through network groups, face-to-face marketing more than anything else. You can do it through the web as well, but I've found that face-to-face networking works much better for this system.

We're going to go over several things in this section. We're going to:

- Look at what a referral is
- Define the two types of referrals
- Show three basic ways of getting referrals
- Describe the three basic kinds of networking groups
- Discuss how to network within those groups
- Warn about which groups not to sell to
- And, of course, how to get more referrals

At the end I'm even going to give you the number one tip: The most important thing you can do to get referrals and it may not be what you think

What is a referral?

EXAMPLE: Daniel is a plumber. Mary has bursting pipes in her house and her house is filled with water. Daniel and Mary happen to be in a networking group together, so she calls Daniel and asks for him to come over right away.

That is a sale or a transaction, not a referral.

EXAMPLE: Mary doesn't have any plumbing issues right now, but she knows a remodeler named John. John needs a certified plumber to help on a job. Mary gives Daniel's information to John and John's information to Daniel. That is a referral. In fact, that's what I call a hot referral. So remember, selling directly to the people in a group, even a referral networking group, is not a referral; it's a sale. Even if those people are potentially your customers, it's still not a referral (some groups do call those "internal referrals").

Two Kinds of Referrals

We've talked about what a referral is so now let's look at the two basic kinds of referrals. Some people say there are three: Cold, warm, and hot. I don't call the cold kind referrals. To me, a cold referral is advertising. It is an ad on a website, on a blog, a cold call on a phone or something like that.

Warm referrals

EXAMPLE: You and a friend are talking one day when your friend says that they are dreading getting an oil change in their car the next time. The garage where they currently go takes forever, stinks, and they only show daytime soaps on the television (you get the drift). You happen to have the card of a mechanic shop that is offering free oil changes for new customers, so you give the card to your friend.

That is a warm referral.

The reason it is a warm referral is twofold: Your friend does not need an oil change at this moment and, although he/she is complaining, they may keep going to the old place anyway. The second reason this is a warm referral is because you did not call the auto shop and tell them your friend would be coming in.

Hot Referrals

But what if your friend does need an oil change now? The way to make this warm referral into a hot referral is to call your auto shop and tell them that your friend will be in to get their oil changed soon. Now your friend has their card and the auto shop is expecting him or her.

A hot referral depends on three specific things:

- The person needs the product or service now.
- The company has the product/service available (or can get it quickly).
- You have communicated with both the potential customer and the company.

Three Types of Networking Groups

There are actually many more than three types of networking groups. These are broad-stroke types to give you an idea of what to look for. There's:

- Social networking
- Chamber of Commerce
- Referral networking

Social Networking

A social networking group is, like the name implies, a social group. Social networking groups are generally made up of people that have similar interests, but are not necessarily getting together to do business. Rotary International, Kiwanis, and Lions are good examples of social clubs.

People in these particular clubs join so they can volunteer their time (and/or money) toward a worthy cause. These clubs have regular meetings, and business people may get referrals, but that is not the purpose of the club. In fact, *you may be asked to leave a social networking group if you continually try to sell to your fellow members.*

Chamber of Commerce

A Chamber of Commerce is a combination of social networking, referral networking, direct selling, and small business advocacy. The purpose of local Chambers of Commerce is to help business owners network and grow.

Chambers of Commerce generally have meetings or luncheons on current topics that may be political or business-oriented. These meetings are designed to educate the members, offer a social avenue, and be a place to network your business. Both direct sales and asking for referrals are encouraged.

If you sell directly to the people in social networking groups, there is a chance you might get asked to leave the group. Chamber of Commerce is almost expected that you sell to each other.

Referral Networking Groups

A referral networking group is the group you don't sell to; you sell through. This type of group is all about referrals, not sales. That rule applies even if every person in the group is a potential customer. Members of referral networking groups do not generally like being sold to by other members; so you may be asked to leave if you continually do so.

Recap:

Social networking groups: Generally, do not try to sell to the people or ask for referrals unless you specifically hear of an opportunity (someone tells you they need your services).

Chambers of Commerce: Sell and refer. Sell more, refer more.

Referral networking groups: No direct selling, but give and get as many referrals as you can.

Getting Referrals

There are three basic ways to ask for referrals from networking groups. They are:

1 to 1 Meetings
Presentations
Elevator Speeches

1 to 1 Meetings

The 1 to 1 meeting is generally where two business people sit down for about an hour and talk. Luckily for introverts, this is not a social hour. The purpose of this talk is so you can learn about the other person, their business, and how you can best refer potential clients to them.

You generally split the time in half (beware of hogging the limelight; make sure you each have equal time) and each of you talks about:

- Who you are

- What you do
- Why you do it
- Most importantly, what's the best referral for you

That last point is huge. I can't tell you how many 1 to 1's I've been on where I walked away and realized that I didn't know who a good referral was for the other person. By the way, just in case you are wondering, your prime referral is the same as your target market. As I described in **_Leadership for Introverts_** (and you may not have read it if you are an extrovert), your target market should be so exact that you can even describe the clothes that person is most likely to wear.

The 1 to 1 approach can be used in any networking situation. You could even use this approach with a person you meet in a checkout line of a grocery store. The other person doesn't even have to have their own small business. Simply ask the other person if they would like to get coffee (juice, lunch, etc.) so you two can learn more about each other's business/work.

EXAMPLE: Jackie specializes in writing resumes and she is awesome. She has determined that her target market is students finishing college. She could do 1 to 1's with college students with the goal of paying for referrals they would give to her. And the 1 to 1 would also give her a better idea if that particular person would be a good fit to give referrals.

Remember: People are 10 times more likely to do business with people they know, like, and trust. 1 to 1's are a great way to do all three of those.

Presentations

Presentations, in general, are eight to ten minute periods of time where you have a captive audience. You have the opportunity to talk about your business to the entire group without interruption (you can have a Q&A session at the end if you want).

A good presentation would be a shortened version of your 1 to 1. Remember, a 1 to 1 is about 30 minutes for each person. Use the same talking points as a 1 to 1:

- Who you are
- What you do
- Why you do it
- Most importantly, what's the best referral for you

But shorten each so you can fit it all into 8-10 minutes.

Do your presentations in whatever way works for you. Here is my way of conducting an eight-minute presentation, in case you have not done one before and would like ideas:

- Minutes 1-4: I take the first four minutes to talk about what I do and why I do it. I very briefly explain who I am (I'm more interested in people knowing what I do and why I do it; your why will show your passion, that can be very important).
- Minutes 5-6: I then spent in about two minutes talking about what the best referrals are for me. I try to be as specific as possible.

- Minutes 7-8: The last two minutes I spend on a Q&A session. This is up to you, but it can help you get more referrals. Answering questions about your type of business will show you as an authority.

The Q&A session can give you an advantage even if you do not know the answers to some questions. Being an authority does not necessarily mean you have all the answers, but you can get them. If you don't know the answer to a question someone asks you; look them straight in the eye with a smile on your face and say: "That is an excellent question; I will get back to you on that." And then get back to them as soon as possible. You will establish trust by getting back to them (how often has someone told you they would do something, then never done it? How much do you trust them?).

They will trust you more because you remembered what they said and you got back to them. Call them, send an email, or contact them on social media. The medium does not matter, just contact them.

Presentations work best in referral networking groups, although you may also have the opportunity to present at some Chamber of Commerce meetings. Speaking about your business in front of the group rarely, if ever, happens at social networking events unless you are paying to play.

Elevator Speeches

The term is called an elevator speech because you want to keep it short, as if you had only the time between two floors in an elevator to explain what you do. I also recommend creating an Edict. And yes, if you read **Leadership for Introverts**, you already know what an Edict is. For those who have unfortunately not read it *yet*, I will explain edicts in just a bit.

Your elevator speech is the most important thing that you can do to help your business in getting referrals, or even getting people to know about you. Spend time crafting your elevator speech until you can explain exactly what you do in one minute or less.

Your elevator speech should contain who you are, what you do, why you do what you do and your target referral. If your chest is tightening just thinking about doing that in under a minute, breathe; it's not something you have to perfect this minute.

EXAMPLE: "Hi, I'm Jim. I'm a backyard entertainment transformation specialist. I work with XYZ Construction Company. We help people turn their backyard into a relaxation station. We can build decks and patios, put in a Jacuzzi surround and much more. We work with all sizes of budgets, and we offer a free estimate. A great referral for me would be a neighbor that's always commenting on how they would like a better back yard for themselves, to entertain and/or their family. You can contact me at my phone number or web site."

Notice that Jim did not start with something like "I do construction." The beginning of your elevator speech is a good place to be creative. "I am a backyard entertainment transformation specialist." It begs people to ask what he means by that; it's a conversation starter.

The Edict

In fact, that could be his Edict. An edict is what you do in six words or less. To give you an idea, an Edict for Nike could be "athletic apparel." McDonald's could be "fast food." Wendy's could be "healthier fast food."

Think of an Edict as what you could say about what your business does in the time it takes to shake someone's hand.

Summary

So far, we've gone over the three types of groups:

- Social groups
- Chambers of commerce
- Referral networking groups

And we've gone over three terms:

- 1 to 1's
- Presentations
- Elevator speech (and Edict)

I also talked about how you do not generally want to sell directly to members of your referral networking and social groups (you may naturally get sales over time, but don't push it). And I know I said it before but it is important that you do not specifically sell, especially hard sell, to a referral networking group. Your best case scenario will be that nobody will ever give a referral to you; worst case, you may be asked to leave. So remember to sell through those people, don't sell to them.

Beginning Networking for Introverts

Visualize the last meeting you went to; you saw a table or tables of people when you walked through the doors. How did you feel? Did your chest tighten up? Did your breath start to get short? Did doubt start to enter your mind? Were you wondering if you still had a chance to run away, or did someone already see you?

I've been there and I've done that. I still feel that way sometimes, so let's do a quick exercise. This is a physical exercise that will change your mental state (do this at a place where you can be alone. Go to the bathroom if you cannot find anywhere else). Take a deep breath in while you hug yourself and then I want you to throw your arms out while you breathe out and smile a huge smile.

I know, you have probably done something like this before if you have ever gone to a positive motivational seminar. But please do this. In fact, try it right now (go to the bathroom if you have to).

Yes, you can hide from me and use all the same excuses I used in the past, like:

- This is stupid. I'm not going to make a fool out of myself (you are alone; the only person who will see is you).
- I will do it "mentally" (come on, that's a cop-out and you know it).
- I will do it next chance I get (no, you won't, so do it now).
- But that's not "me" (and that's the point. I want to get you out of your "normal" introvert self).

So let's do this once real quick: arms tight hugging yourself, breathe in. Now breathe out with a big smile on your face while throwing your arms wide open. Notice how you already feel calmer, more centered and more focused?

Use this visualization technique the next time you're going to walk into a referral networking group. You've done your hugging technique and you have your elevator speech down. You open that door, walk in calm and centered and you look at that table or tables full of people. I want you to look at those people for who they are: They are your sales force.

They are there to sell for you as much as you are to sell for them. Now, doesn't that make you feel a little bit calmer? Think about it; you're taking your time to make sure that they know how to sell for you. So your 60-second elevator speech has to include helping your sales force learn how to best refer sales to you this week. And I explain just how to do that in the next chapter.

202 - Advanced Networking

I have been doing referral networking for over 20 years and through much of that time I received very few referrals. It was very frustrating and I had a difficult time. I would stop going to groups for long periods of time; there was even a year where I decided not to do referral networking anymore at all. I felt it wasn't worth it at the time because I wasn't getting more than one referral every three to five months. Unless you sell a very high-end product that is simply not enough to justify all the time and money it takes to do referral networking.

I couldn't figure out why I received so few referrals. I spent many hours developing my elevator speech, 1 to 1 technique, and presentations (all described in the 101 section).

After more years than I care to admit, I realized there were two simple reasons why I was not getting more referrals: I wasn't *giving* many referrals, and I wasn't *asking* for referrals.

Giving Referrals

There's one trick to getting more referrals consistently and, if done right, you can be terrible at networking and still be super successful. That trick is to give more referrals. One sure-fire way to get other business owners to know, like and trust you is to give them referrals. Giving them a referral tells them that you trust them, so they will automatically want to trust you more.

So the next time you go into your referral group, Chamber of Commerce meeting or even social group, go in with at least two or three referrals. Try to get referrals to different people each time and give as many referrals as you can.

But don't fake it. Give real referrals. People will catch on quick if your referrals don't pan out.

> I stepped into a referral marketing group early one morning. It was a paid group that met weekly. One of the requirements was to give a certain number of referrals each month.

"I have a referral for you!" Jenny said enthusiastically.

She handed me a sheet of paper with a name and number scribbled on it.

"They desperately need your help," she said. "Their web site is out of date and they can't be found on the search engines."

"Thank you so much!" I responded. "Are they expecting my call?"

"Well, no. But look at their web site, it's terrible, they need your help," she said.

That is not a referral; I'm not sure if it's even a lead. And it definitely didn't make me want to trust her. Give real referrals.

A real referral, as I talked about in the 101 section, is a person *you've already talked to* that needs and wants the products and services the other person offers. Read "What Is a Referral, Two kinds of referrals" in the 101 section if you haven't yet.

You want to give others a hot referral; just like you would want a hot referral from them. The more referrals you give; the more people are going to want to give referrals to you. But even better; the more referrals you give, the more immediate the know, like and trust happens because you're telling them you're already trusting them with people that you know. That is a great way to get more referrals.

Asking For Referrals

One reason I wasn't getting referrals because I didn't know how to ask for them. A great way to get more referrals is to say something like: "The best referral for me is..." or "a good referral for me is..."

Those are great terms to use, but there is a fundamental problem with them; those terms do not ask a question. And why is a question important?

Think of this: You are exchanging information with a referral partner and they say a good referral for them is a person who is looking for a home. You politely nod your head and file the information away, hoping you will remember it later. You may or may not think of a person you know who is looking for a home right now, but since the other person didn't actually ask for the referral, *your brain isn't trying to figure out a problem.*

We can do better. In coaching, questions are the answer; but they have to be the right questions. You can use specialized coaching questions right now to help you ask the right questions to get those exploding referrals.

So who is your customer? Who's your target client? Are you sure that's your target? You need to ask those questions to make sure you get referrals for the right type of people.

If you are in real estate, it's not much use to go to a homeless person and say "how would you like to be in a million-dollar home tomorrow?" Chances are they don't have the money to do that and the only way for them to get into a million-dollar home might be illegal. You want to find your right customer and ask the right customer the right questions. So what is the right question?

Who do you know?

That's the right question. Who do you know? Write that down. Those are the four most important words that you can use in getting exploding referrals. If a plumber says "a good referral for me is a person with a clogged toilet;" okay, the other people write down "anybody with a clogged toilet."

If you are lucky, they will dutifully write it down before turning their attention to the next person. So let's switch that: Plumber; "who do you know that has a clogged toilet or the toilet gets clogged all the time? Think of a specific name. Would you contact that person in the next couple of days and give them my information, or ask them if I can have their contact information?"

You just got exploding referrals. Do you see how asking the right questions will make others think of specific people rather than generalities? You just changed it from "anybody that might have a clogged toilet" to someone else in your referral group thinking "wow, wait a minute. John talked about his toilet being clogged all the time. I remember that. I'll contact John."

Do you see how simple it is (of course, it wasn't simple before you knew it, was it)? Who do you know? Who do you know that could benefit from this type of information? Have you seen other people struggling with getting referrals? Think of one or two people in your referral group that could use this and tell them about this book. Or, send them to **www.explodingreferrals.com**. That's how easy it is. But don't wait until the next time you see them, email or message them now; send them a link to the book and tell them how helpful it's been for you.

Think of four or five "who do you know" questions and categorize them. Let's say you are a real estate agent. What are four questions you could ask? "Who do you know that is tired of living in an apartment? Who do you know that has kids going off to college?" You get the point, think of one or two more.

But always remember the next step. "Think of a specific person. Will you contact them and ask if I can have their information?" THAT, my friend, is a HOT referral.

I have my questions written down and laminated (yes, I'm detailed like that... when I want to be). That way the piece of paper doesn't get wrinkled, crinkled and end up looking terrible. Better yet, make a document on an electronic tablet. That way you can change your questions without much trouble.

Now, in a 1 to 1, you can go in and ask those questions. You have a half hour to create a thorough presentation about what you do and why you do it. But always save time at the end for your Exploding Referral questions.

Be careful with this if you are doing a one to one with a person you don't know well. If you do a one to one with a new referral partner, and start bombarding them with these questions, they may think you are being very pushy and not trust you.

Referral marketing is relationships, relationships, relationships. Okay, it's a bit more than that; it is a combination of relationships and transactions. The relationship is getting to know the people so they can like and trust you more. The transaction is asking for the referral. But don't bombard the people with a bunch of questions if you don't have a relationship with them.

I learned that the hard way when I first started doing this. I was very excited about the process, so the next 1 to 1 I asked 10 "who do you know" questions. And I had my tablet ready to write down the first name of each person she was going to give me.

But that 1 to 1 was with a person I didn't know well. She didn't give me a single name and the meeting didn't end well.

Luckily she was a very nice person; she understood once I explained to her why I was bombarding her. But don't do that with someone you don't know well. The better you know somebody, the more questions you can ask (but don't go above five or six). If you don't know them at all I would recommend one to two questions at the most. You may even decide to wait until the next 1 to 1 to ask for exploding referrals if you have never met the person before.

Think of three to five questions you can use throughout your 8-10 minute presentations. And be sure to ask them to think of a specific person who is currently having that problem.

EXAMPLE: Julie does multi-level marketing with a cosmetics company. Good questions for her might be: "Who do you know that is a military wife?" Military wives move around a lot, so it would benefit them to be part of something that can move with them. "Who do you know that wants to make an extra $$$ each month?" "Who do you know that is earth-conscious?" Of course, she would only want to say this if the company where she works does not test on animals.

You get the idea. She could even start with "Our products are never tested on animals. Who do you know…"

Ask each listener to write down the name of one specific person. Then, at the end of the presentation, pass around your business cards and ask them to contact that person for you.

You may not want to ask "who do you know" questions on four different subjects. EXAMPLE: A real estate agent does an 8-minute presentation to his group. He asks six "who do you know" questions during the presentation and the questions range from a person who wants to buy a house, a college student looking for a rental apartment, empty-nesters looking to downsize, etc.

We all want as many clients as we can get, but you don't want to confuse your audience. Be as specific as you can. Keep your audience on one subject and they will start to think about people who are looking for that specific service. You can always talk on a different subject next time.

The Power Question

One way to captivate your audience is to come up with one power question. Design a speech around one specific aspect of your business, and ask one power question several times.

EXAMPLE: "Who do you know that wants to transform their back yard into an entertainment oasis? My company builds decks that have fireplaces, barbecues, retractable awnings, and more. So who do you know that would like that type of oasis in their back yard? Think of one specific person you know that might be interested, I'm going to pass out my business card. Would you write their name on the back of my card and contact them? I would love to see if we would be a good fit for that friend of yours who loves to entertain."

That is powerful. You have just painted a Monet in their mind of your target audience (although I am sure you could do better than I). And you can change your power question each time you meet with that group or with each different group. You may change your power question with the season, or during special events. Or stick to one power question if it is generating hot referrals.

Magazines and phone books were the big things in advertising back in the days before the internet. And advertisers warned people that you needed to get your ad in front of a person, on average, 20 times before they would even think about your product or service. So just about the time you're getting tired of saying it; your audience is getting it. And it's the same thing with asking these questions.

You may want to ask the same question over and over to solidify it for your referral partners. In fact, if you do that, create a game out of it. After you've asked the same question several times, over weeks or months, give a gift card to the first person who remembers it.

Personally, I change my power question every couple of weeks; or I might change it depending on the group I meet. That's the advantage of having 1-5 questions written down. Your power question might be question number three on your list for one group and question number five in another group. Or it might not be part of your 1-5 questions at all. Read the group and think about what would resonate with them the most.

WARNING: Don't make your questions too generic. As I mentioned, a person who sells beauty products shouldn't say "who do you know that has skin?" Be as specific as you can. The more specific you are, the more likely you're going to get exploding referrals.

Just like your target market, the more specific you are with your question the more likely you're going to hit that target.

Super-Secret Squirrel

You made it to the Super-Secret Squirrel area. Here are some tips on how to use "Who do you know" in unique and different ways.

Like I said before, you do not, do not, do not want to sell directly to referral networks and social networks. BUT, there is a super-secret squirrel way to sell to these people.

EXAMPLE: A commercial plumber is in a referral networking group with a property manager. The property manager has 15 properties and they are constantly having plumbing issues. The commercial plumber is probably foaming at the mouth for a chance to sell to this person.

So the plumber schedules a 1 to 1 with the property manager. At the beginning of the meeting, the plumber could say something like: "I know you could be a potential customer, but I'm sure you know other property managers. So do not feel pressured to do business with me. Everything I'm going to tell you will be so you have the information to tell others about me." That should alleviate any unease the property manager would have about being sold to.

That's the trick. In fact, if you use the "who do you know" to a person like the property manager, they will know you are not trying to sell to them. Give them the opportunity to make themselves your customer.

Another secret: There's a way to get referrals without ever opening your mouth. Okay introverts, I know you are really looking forward to this one. I'm an introvert myself. I had a tough time asking for referrals, but it's been much easier since I figured this out.

So how do you get a referral without ever opening your mouth? Well if you are in business, especially a small business or service-oriented business, you should have a business card. If you don't, get some. Every small business person that needs referrals needs business cards to hand out to referral partners.

Now, you might ask "why do I need to hand out my business card to these people? They already have one; they know who I am..." etc., etc. It's okay, bring all the excuses out. Then think about where you put their business cards? Did you dutifully file them for easy access? Most of them didn't. They would be lucky to know where your card is, if they even have it anymore.

Each of your referral partners should have a couple of your cards, but here's the trick: business cards can also be purchased at your local office supply store and online. No, I'm not talking about customized cards, but blank ones you can print yourself.

Print out your power question so the next time you go to your referral group, you don't even need to say "who do you know." Just hand out the card that has your power question and contact information. It's going to be difficult for them to forget your power question because they're taking it home with them and they're going to be looking at it thinking about who they can refer to you.

If your group goes around the room with 60-second commercials, you could just stand up and you say: "I'm not going to give a commercial today; I'm going to hand out my card and the card says everything." this is a great way of getting referrals without saying a word.

The #1 Way to Get Exploding Referrals

Remember, you're going to get more referrals when three things happen; when the person knows, likes and trusts you. So what if you are new to networking? Well, unless you are new in business, there is one other way you can get exploding referrals. In fact, it is the #1 way to do it: Use the "who do you know" technique with your past customers. These people already know, like and trust you because they have already purchased your products or services.

So contact your past customers. Call them, send an email, use smoke signals or whatever it takes. Offer an incentive if they refer someone who signs with you. Or, better yet, offer an incentive for both them and the referral. You could offer a free consultation, a sample of your products (by the way, if you sell Lexus's, I would be happy to have a sample).

Sending an incentive for a referral is a great trick, but it's not a trick at all. It actually tells the person that you respect their referral. And when they feel that way, they will like and trust you more. So, if nothing else, send them a thank you card. Not an email, an actual card. And sign it.

Conclusion

Are you a little stumped on the right questions to ask? It's okay; it can be difficult to get them just right and specific enough. Like I said, the beauty consultant doesn't want to say "who do you know that has skin?" They want to say: "who do you know that's always fighting acne?" if they have a product that solves that. Be specific, not general.

And if you are stumped, give us a holler at **www.portbell.com**. We can help you with "Who do you know" questions.

Who do you know that could benefit from the tips in this book? Can you think of one or two people that want to get more referrals? Send them to **www.explodingreferrals.com** so they can gain more customers also.

www.ingramcontent.com/pod-product-compliance
Lightning Source LLC
Chambersburg PA
CBHW030037230526
45472CB00002B/550